# STILL I RISE

&

# MANAGE DEPRESSION

*Learn to Live a Balanced Life with Mental Illness*

GARRY L. JONES

Copyright © 2016 by Garry L. Jones

VMH

*VMH Vikki M. Hankins™ Publishing*
3355 Lenox Rd. NE Suite 750
Atlanta, GA 30326
www.vmhpublishing.com

Without limiting the rights under copyright reserved above, no part of this publication may be reproduced, stored in or introduced into a retrieval system, or transmitted, in any form or by any means, without prior written permission of both the copyright owner and publisher of this book. Your support of the author's rights is appreciated.

*Manufactured in the United States of America*

Hardback ISBN: 978-0-9984553-4-1
Paperback ISBN: 978-0-9984553-2-7

10 9 8 7 6 5 4 3 2 1

Author's Note:

The names and characters have been changed to protect the privacy of such individual's. The events documented in this publication are according to the author's memory. Further, the author is not a doctor nor a psychologist, but instead shares personal experiences.

*The publisher is not responsible for websites, or social media pages (or their content) that are not owned by the publisher.*

*Mental health related issues do not discriminate; it affects men and women as well as the rich and the poor.*

# CHAPTER

# 1

*The Day I Was Born*

I was born to a sixteen-year-old mother on January 25, 1964. I don't know what the atmosphere was like, considering my mother was staying with my grandparents as well as seven siblings. If you count my brother, Pete, who was born eleven months prior to me, and throw in a cousin, who would become a sister to me, I would consider this to be a crowded house. As a matter of fact, if my math is correct, this comes out to be a total of thirteen people living in a four-bedroom apartment. Within two years, the total was fifteen people staying in the four-bedroom apartment because my sister, Lisa, and my youngest brother, Junior, were born.

Up until I was five years old, I was having a ball. I can't say this about my five aunts and two uncles because my mother was running the streets. My uncles and aunts duties were to help raise my siblings and me. I had wonderful grandparents - a grandmother who fussed a great deal and a grandfather who let us do what we wanted to do. Life was fantastic. I was excited when I used to be under my granddaddy, and whatever my granddaddy said was the law. My grandmother would intervene and say, "Alright, Wesley, you don't need to have those grandchildren in the car while you are out drinking." I think this fell on deaf ears because my granddaddy would do the reverse. My grandmother, Tessie, meant well, and later on in life, I would become the apple of her eye. I know my grandmother and granddaddy had to be saying, "How in the hell are we going to be able to raise these grandchildren when it is already hard enough putting food on the table for the eight we already have?"

In my grandparents' eyes, we never felt anything other than love. There was no indication that my siblings and I were a mistake. Most of the time, when you already have a large family and unexpected babies come along, it causes financial hardship in the household. I don't know whether this caused my granddaddy to drink a lot, but I'm sure it may have contributed. Every time my granddaddy's automobile would crank, we would go outside and climb up in the automobile. I can recall one time, my grandfather took us with him to pay a bill, and the office was located on a hill. Below that hill was the Neuse River. My granddaddy got out of the automobile and went into the office to pay the insurance bill. He left my siblings, Pete, Lisa, and my cousin, Sharon, and I in the automobile by ourselves. Sharon decided

*Picture of Tessie and me when I was a boy.*

*Older family picture, taken in Washington D.C.*

to grab the shift gear and put the car in reverse by mistake. All of a sudden, the car started rolling backwards and was going down the hill towards the Neuse River. We started screaming, and I don't know where this angel came from, but he ran toward the automobile, jumped in, and put the shift gear back in the park position.

When my granddaddy came out of the office and discovered what happened, he had fear in his eyes. I don't remember exactly what he said, but I'm sure he told us not to tell our grandmother. If we would have told her what happened, it would have been on and popping in the Jones' household. My grandmother didn't play, and she didn't take any mess off of my granddaddy. If that info had been divulged, she would have been fit to be tied - whatever the hell that meant back in those days. People coined a lot of phrases that are used today.

# CHAPTER 2

*1970*
*The Year My Granddaddy Died*

I loved the year 1970. I was either going to the first grade or kindergarten, but nevertheless, I was going to school. At first, I wanted to be at school, and then, all of a sudden, I wanted to be home under my grandmother. I would cry when it was time for me to go to school, but crying didn't faze my grandparents. I could have cried until I was blue in the face. My uncle, Hamm, was ordered to walk us to school. Lewis Elementary School was only four blocks away from the apartment. I think that, during this time, my mother was a dispatcher for one of many taxi services in my hometown. When school was out, a taxi would be waiting to pick my siblings and I up from school and take us home. I didn't like riding home in a taxi; I wanted to walk home with my friends.

*Picture of Daddy (Granddaddy)*

As soon as we walked in the house, we were made to take off our school clothes and do our homework before we were allowed to go out and play. My siblings and I had plenty of help with our homework; I think that my uncle, Jay, was a teacher or guidance counselor, as well as my aunt, Denderaunt. My three oldest aunts, Mary, Jean, and Arnetta, had moved up North, and when my aunt, Denderaunt, and Jay weren't available, my aunt, Mavis, and my cousin, Ann, pitched in to help. I think my mother had gotten married because I can't remember her staying in the house. During this time, my grandfather was ill, and I would often go upstairs to speak with him. I can't recall what the conversation was about, but I used to wonder why he had a patch over his eye. He used to have money and a potato cake on his dresser, and I would say, "Daddy, can I have this? Daddy, can I have that?" He would always say yes. After I got the money off of the dresser, I would run outside to the store.

    I would soon find out that my granddaddy had cancer in the eye, and one of his eyes had been removed. This was the reason he had a patch over one of his eyes. I can recall one night, I was at the house, and there were so many people in my granddaddy's bedroom. The majority of the people were family, and they was either standing up by his bed or sitting down. My grandmother was constantly taking a towel and putting it under his mouth because he was hemorrhaging. I didn't have a clue that my granddaddy was dying, but as I think back now, I know why so many people were at my granddaddy's bedside. Although I was in and out of my granddaddy's room when he was dying, I wasn't listening to the conversation between him and my grandmother. I was told that he made her promise that she would raise my brother and I; we were not to be raised by my mother. Eventually, my brother and I would be called my grandmother's boys, and until this day, that's what some of my grandmother's friends call us - "Tessie's Boys."

I can recall the ambulance picking up my granddaddy and taking him to the funeral home. I would go and visit him two or three times a day. As a matter of fact, I would take my friends to go and visit him. Some may ask why I continued to go to the funeral home to visit my granddaddy so many times. During that time, I didn't comprehend death; to me, my granddaddy was asleep. After the funeral, all of my grandmother's children pitched in to help raise us. We didn't want for anything, and until this day, I can always depend on my aunts and uncles to help me out when I get in a bind. Although my father didn't raise me, I knew who he was, and I would eventually work for him for a short period of time.

ns" />

# CHAPTER 3

*A Strange Feeling Began To Hover Over Me*

**A** couple of months after my grandfather passed, a strange feeling came over me; I began to feel sad for no reason. I can't say that it was because of my granddaddy's death because I only had six years to bond with him, and for the first three years of my life, I can't recall remembering too many things. I was a normal kid who had plenty of friends, food to eat, and when I wanted some spare change, I would hustle bottles and cut grass. The feeling was so heavy that I would often go across the street to a cemetery and cry. Growing up, we were taught not to be a crybaby, so therefore, in order to hide how I was feeling, I would be by myself. Sometimes, I would go upstairs and go to sleep, hoping that when I awakened, that sad feeling would be gone. Although I was six years old, I wasn't required to come in the house to take a nap; I only had to do this when I was at school. As a matter of fact, if we stayed in the house too long, we were made to go outside and play.

We couldn't sit around the house unless we were sick or we were cleaning house. I felt better when I played basketball, dodge ball, or a pickup game of football. If I wasn't playing on the playground, I would go to the recreation center where music was played all day while others shot pool, played ping pong, or played spades. I had plenty of friends, but my best friend's name was Antray. I knew that I could share anything with him, but telling your friend that you felt like crying was not an option. It was embedded in our heads not to be a crybaby, and if some of the older cats saw you crying, they would say, "Wipe those damn tears or carry your ass home. Shake it off; men don't cry." I wanted to say, "I'm not a man; I'm a boy," but I was taught not to talk back to our elders at an early age, so I had to suck it up.

There were times that I was able to cry and get away with it either at school or at home. I was born with asthma, so most of the time, I couldn't breathe, and when I was diagnosed with ulcers, my stomach would hurt all the time. When I was sick or had a pretty bad fall, it was okay to cry because that was a pretty good reason. When an individual was hurting mentally, at a young age, it's very confusing. Most of the time when I was hurting and my family knew I was hurting, they would ask, "Where are you hurting?" I didn't know how to tell my family and friends that I was hurting on the inside. How can you express that your mind is hurting in the seventies, especially when you don't know what the hell is going on?

Can you imagine going around telling people that your mind is hurting and that's the reason you are crying? Not only would you be considered a crybaby, but growing up in my neighborhood, they would have told me that I must have lost my damn mind! I can't imagine; I would have been taken to a doctor because children's minds don't hurt - or so they thought.

Later on in life, I would learn that there was something wrong with me, and you don't have to be an adult to have mental anguish.

# CHAPTER 4

*Masking the Pain at An Early Age*

After I realized that I couldn't express my thoughts to people, I had to mask the pain. As I mentioned earlier, when I was feeling this pain, I would often go to the cemetery across the street from where I lived and shed some tears or take a nap, hoping when I awakened, the pain would have gone away. For a long time in my life, this would become a norm - taking naps or going to the cemetery to shed some tears. I didn't know where the pain was coming from, but I knew it wasn't normal. In order for me to keep from crying in front of people, the Lord blessed me with a beautiful smile; at least, that is what some people said. Sometimes, I couldn't feel anything; I just went through the routine of living.

When taking naps and shedding tears no longer eased the pain, I discovered that if I stayed busy, playing with my friends, looking at television, and making a hustle, the pain would go away. I knew at an early age that being alone and keeping everything on the inside, I would eventually break down.

Although I kept a smile on my face, I was dying on the inside, but that smile kept people from asking me how I felt. The smile on my face indicated that I was a happy young man with no worries in the world. My friends and I would go to the movies after attending church. We stayed at the movies all day on Sunday. In the early 70's, I was exposed to black exploitation movies, movies such as *Super Fly*, *Hell up in Harlem*, *Three the Hard Way*, *Black Caesar*, *Foxy Brown*, *Slaughter*, *Dolomite*, *Hit Man*, *The Black Six*, *Black Shampoo*, and many more movies. I was still a child, and as a child, I did enjoy movies like *Jaws*, *Jaws 2*, *Enter the Dragon*, *Fist of Fury*, and *ET*.

During the week, my Uncle Jay kept me busy, emphasizing that education was the key if I wanted to succeed in life. I had to study, and if I didn't do my homework, going outside to play wasn't an option. Doing homework was hard because, when I ran into a problem that I couldn't solve, I would get frustrated. The sadness would set in, and I wanted to cry because I couldn't concentrate. I wasn't a dumb kid because I made good grades, and that was because I worked hard at it, and I had family to help me with my work.

When my Uncle Jay and my grandmother said that it was okay to go outside and play, I ran out the door as fast as I could. That was my relief. I could breathe, and I didn't have to worry about hyperventilating. My Uncle Jay would eventually come outside and gather up a group of boys, and he taught us how to play sports.

I was becoming an expert on masking the pain I felt on the inside. I still didn't have a clue what was going on with me. I knew that the sad feeling on the inside was not normal.

# CHAPTER

# 5

*I Think I Figured Out
What Was Wrong*

As I got older, I began to figure out what was wrong with me. I was still in school, but I still had those same sad feelings. My activities didn't change, but I became wiser. I was still participating in sports.

Although I made decent grades in school, it was hard for me to articulate and comprehend what I read. I loved sports with all of my heart and soul, and when I tried out for school sports, it was hard for me to remember my plays, and sometimes I couldn't articulate my thoughts when I was trying to convey what I was saying. Although it was hard for me to remember my plays, I was still good enough to make the team. I played basketball, football, and ran track.

As I got older, I would began to realize what I was going through, but I wasn't sure because if I shared it with anyone I knew, I would get teased as being sick in the head. As a matter of fact, I would tease people who the community said was sick in the head. Like I said earlier, I wouldn't dare share it with anyone, and one day when I was in high school, I went to my family physician. On this particular day, I told my grandmother that she didn't have to accompany me to the examining room. When I walked back to get examined, I shared something with my doctor; I told him that I felt like crying all of the time but for no reason. He asked me how long I had been feeling this way, and I said as early as six years old. The doctor said, "I think you may be suffering from depression."

I knew what depression was, but when he said that he was going to send me to a psychiatrist, I declined, left the office abruptly, and didn't say anything to my grandmother. This was one secret that I would keep for the rest of my life, so I thought. Throughout high school, I was dating, but it didn't last long because my feelings didn't last long for any woman; I felt numb on the inside. The doctor, who recommended that I go to visit a psychiatrist, committed suicide years later.

# CHAPTER 6

*Self-Medicating In College*

When I went off to college, I continued to feel depressed and hopeless although I was popular. I began to drink, sniff cocaine, and smoke marijuana to numb the pain. Drugs were all around me, and as a matter of fact, I don't remember paying for any drugs, but the depression was getting worse. I had to give up marijuana because when I smoked it, I became paranoid. I could feel myself losing it. It was only a matter of time before I lost my mind, but going to see a psychiatrist was not the answer for me. When I was a sophomore in college, my father gave me a car to drive. I felt good temporarily, although I wasn't making wise decisions. Sometimes, I would drink before I went to class to numb the pain, and I no longer had sports to turn to because I decided not to play college ball. Going to visit other colleges and partying was the thing to do, but most of the time when I went, I was drinking. It is amazing and through the grace of God that I didn't kill myself or anyone else because I couldn't put the alcohol down.

I had a girlfriend that I had started dating on a regular basis in my hometown. One day, when I was home, I confided in her that I was suffering from depression, but she brushed it off as if to say that everyone goes through that from time to time. I immediately shut down; from that day forward, I made a promise that I wouldn't tell anyone what I was going through. I found myself getting in fights; this was not normal for me. I was easy to get along with. My girlfriend was pregnant, and I was feeling the pressure of raising a child because I was taught never to neglect my responsibilities.

Five weeks prior to receiving my criminal justice degree, I was gunned down in a nightclub. How in the hell was I going to take care of my nine month old daughter, having sustained an injury that affected my nerves, leaving me in a great deal of pain? This made things worse for me because I was now in mental anguish and suffering from sciatic nerve problems. I begin to drink heavily, but I was still working out with the weights, trying to keep my body in shape. Eventually, the drugs and alcohol weren't doing the job; I couldn't get any relief for my depression.

# CHAPTER

7

*My First Job After College*

It was November 1986, and I had gotten myself back in shape physically to go work. I was still in a lot of pain from the gunshot wounds, but I had to seek employment to take care of my family. I was employed at a place called Nova Behavior Center in my hometown. Nova Behavior Center was a place dedicated to building a future and hope for children, adolescents, and adults with concurrent diagnoses by providing individualized services in a highly structured and therapeutic treatment environment. Nova addressed a service need for difficult to place children with emotional, social, and intellectual challenges. Basically, they secured residential care for children with mental illness. In other words, whenever the parents and the school system couldn't handle the children with mental and emotional problems, they would enroll them at Nova.

The government paid a portion for each child Nova housed. I was employed as a teaching parent part-time, working on the weekends from 8:00a.m to 8:00p.m. It was rough working at Nova because the children were uncontrollable at times. I was a young twenty-two year old, who was in pretty good shape. Whenever a student would attack me, I had to take them down by any means necessary. These were some of the strongest children in the world. The children would pick up anything that wasn't tied down and hit you with it. The students took classes during the day, and the teaching parent would cook for them, watch movies with them, and allow them to participate in recreational activities.

Although the students were rough, I realized early on that they needed love; they needed someone to listen and talk with them. The only thing different from me, as an employee, was that the students knew that they suffered from mental and emotional illnesses; they didn't have a problem talking about their issues. I hid my issues and refused to talk about them. Eventually, the students would come to love me because I was easy to get along with. They knew that they couldn't cross the lines with me. They knew that I would give them what they were allowed to have and maybe give them some extra dessert, but I gave the others the same thing. Although I loved some students more than others, I didn't show any favoritism. Showing favoritism would make some students feel less than and could cause their conditions to get worse. Sometimes they would start acting out. Some would find something to cut their wrists with, beat their heads against the wall, and lash out at the kids that were getting the most attention.

When I left work, I was tired and exhausted, and the only thing I could do was go home, play with my children, and get into bed. Eventually, I would get hired full-time, and if I wanted to, I could easily work fifty-six hours a week. Most of the times I did. Later on in life, I would come to find out that without the proper rest and diet, I would fall in a deep state of depression. I only stayed at Nova for eight months before I moved to Washington, D.C. and started a career with the D.C. Department of Corrections.

# CHAPTER 8

*Working in a Stressful Environment Exacerbated My Illness*

The year was 1987, and I began my career with the D.C. Department of Corrections in Washington, D.C., working at the Central Facilities in Lorton, Virginia. I was still in a lot of physical pain from my shooting injuries, and I refused to deal with my mental issues. I was like a walking time bomb. Some say that the place I was employed at had the worse inmates in the United States. To me, this didn't constitute a conflict because people were people to me. Emotionally, I couldn't feel anything, so therefore, I didn't have any fear, and maybe that was a good thing.

I prided myself on coming to work on time and making sure that I dressed appropriately. I was trying my best to keep up that façade, as if everything was okay with me emotionally; I didn't show any weakness. No one had a clue how depressed I was. Most of the time, people envision a person who suffers from mental illness as a person who walks around not well groomed, wearing tacky clothing, and with a somber look on their face. You will be amazed that the people who wear their three piece suits, look good, and walk around with their briefcases are some of the most miserable people in the world, but society has painted a picture of what depression looks like, and it is not that nice looking man or woman who we think has it all together. Those are the same people who are ready to go out and commit suicide because it takes too much energy to hide what you feel on the inside.

There weren't too many days that I worked without either witnessing a stabbing or hearing about someone being stabbed to death on the shift before. I was involved in a lot of fights, and I can't remember losing any of them. I just knew that when I was fighting, I didn't have anything to lose, and when a person came towards me in a threatening manner, I took the fight to them. I was still traumatized from the year before when I was gunned down in a nightclub, and when my space was invaded, I became paranoid and snapped. After the fight was over with, it was back to normal for me. My mind wasn't together, but the inmates didn't know it. I had become numb from witnessing the sexual assaults, stabbings, and hearing about guns being inside the prison. I could see the fear that were in other inmate's eyes concerning whether or not they were going to make it out of prison alive.

When I left work, I would turn to the bottle. I wasn't doing any illegal drugs at the time because we were subject to random drug testing. Alcohol was legal, so I drank the hell out of it. I didn't have enough sense to know that the job was stressful. Sometimes, a person can be under a lot of stress and not know it because working in stressful environments can become the norm; but eventually, your body reacts to the stress and manifests itself in other ways such as losing your hair, being agitated all the time, having problems sleeping, and if you are a woman, it can throw your menstrual cycle off. When I wasn't working, I was traveling to North Carolina a lot to see my girlfriend and children. Although I was suffering from depression, I was determined to not be a deadbeat dad. I would eventually leave Washington D.C. and move back to North Carolina, only to begin work at several more prisons.

# CHAPTER

9

*Uniting With My Family*

After leaving Washington, D.C., I moved back to North Carolina - Raleigh to be exact. I was an hour and a half away from the town I grew up in. This was great, but my girlfriend and my two children weren't staying with me at the time. I took on a job that was less stressful, so I thought. I worked at Triangle, Wake, and Goldsboro Correctional Center, and I had gone from being a Correctional Officer to being a Case Manager. The stress of being a Case Manager was taking its toll. I forgot how many inmates I had on my caseload, but all of them needed attention. When I skimmed through my caseload, I realized that the inmates were behind on the upgrade of their custody level, home leave passes, and work release jobs. The inmate custody level dictated whether or not they would be eligible for home leave and work passes. Let me explain what a custody level is. Upon admission, processing, and evaluation of offenders, they are put through a series of evaluations, including mental and health screening. Prison classification specialists develop an individual profile of each inmate that includes the offender's crime, social background, education, job skills, work history, health, and criminal record prior to his prison sentences.

Based on this information, the offender is assigned to the most appropriate custody classification and prison. The majority of the inmates assigned to me had five years or less on their sentences. An inmate might be in minimum custody, but if they commit an infraction, depending on the severity of the infraction, their custody level may change from minimum custody to medium custody. The job was very stressful because the institution had probably four case managers for one thousand inmates. During this time, I was beginning to feel the weight of the world on my shoulders, plus I was traveling to see my family two or three days a week until I was relocated to an institution closer to my home.

I was under the impression that once I reunited with my family and did less traveling, things would have gotten better, but they didn't. After getting married in 1990 and having another child, my depression got worse. I was home every night and was making money to support my family, but deep down in my soul, I was very depressed. I began to drink again to ease the pain, but I was still working out in the gym. Sometimes, I would drink before I went to the gym; I had to maintain my physique. I may have been drinking like an alcoholic, but I didn't look like one. When I would go to work, I would dress to impress and carry my briefcase. Although I looked like I had it all together, on the inside, I could feel myself losing it. Mental illness does not discriminate whether you are married, single, white, black, Christian, Muslim, rich, poor, or a celebrity. This disease can hit you at anytime, and in some cases, it lies dormant, and it takes a traumatic event to expose it.

# CHAPTER 10

*Getting Closer To Being Exposed*

It was July 16, 1995, my family and I moved to Tallahassee, Florida. I was promoted to Senior Lieutenant, and with the position came major responsibilities. This was double trouble. I had the responsibilities of taking care of my family in a new environment and working at a place that was waiting for my downfall. Working as a Lieutenant came easy to me, but working with your boss, who is determined to make your life a living hell because you weren't his first choice, can put a strain on your mental health. The Captain that I was working for didn't want me in Tallahassee; the warden wanted me there.

Can you imagine going to work in a new environment and having to watch your every move because your supervisor was giving you major assignments to complete without any help? I was informed by my supervisor that I wasn't a team player so therefore he was going to give me a shit load of work. I wasn't the type of person to go along to get along. I didn't like people being treated like dogs and being disrespected because those same people were grown and they had families too. When I would witness staff being disrespected, I would intervene, voice my opinion, and let my supervisor know that what he or she was doing wasn't right. Once you start to balk the system and demand justice, all hell will break loose, and you become a target. My superior began to find ways to get rid of me. Fortunately, I knew how to do my job more so than the supervisors knew how to do their job. The majority of the time I was working the 4:00p.m. shift to the 12:00a.m. shift. The number of Lieutenants needed to adequately run this shift should have been three, but for the majority of the time, I was the only Lieutenant working. Due to the fact that I had a shortage of staff, the chances of me making a mistake was high, but I made it through despite my situation. I had to be sharp on my feet. It was just like playing chess; I had to know or anticipate what the Captain's next move would be. He and the other Captains that came to the institution had the same plan - if we can get Jones to make a mistake, we can discipline him, and the way to get him to make a mistake is to give him the minimum amount of staff to run his shift.

Although I was able to outwit the captains and wardens, it came with a heavy price. The excessive energy I was using to protect myself exacerbated my depression and anxiety. When I left work, I had to deal with a different type of stress - a stress that requires raising your children properly and dealing with a spouse who wants to control your every move. My ex-wife kept pushing God down my throat to the point where I couldn't take it anymore.

# CHAPTER 11

*Reaching Out For Help
Thirty Years Later*

The pressure was getting to me, and I contemplated committing suicide. I could feel my mind leaving me. When I used to go to work prior to me going on the inside, I began to have anxiety. No one could tell because I played it off with a smile, and with the way I was built, there weren't too many people who would try me physically. If I was working the evening shift (4pm to 12pm), I would come home, park in my driveway, and drink my alcohol because I didn't want to go inside the house just to argue. I knew I needed help, so I decided to go see a psychiatrist secretly. I wasn't using any illegal drugs anymore, but I was still drinking heavy. When I would go to workout, I felt the same way when I left – depressed. Working out wasn't easing the pain anymore, and drinking was the only thing that calmed me down. It used to take one drink for me to calm down, but I began to notice that it was taking me five to ten drinks to calm down.

The psychiatrist asked me if I was still drinking, and I told him yes. He told me to stop because he wanted to put me on medication, and if I continued to drink, it would defeat the purpose. I opted to stop drinking and commenced to taking anxiety medication and medication for depression. The medication worked for about a year, and I began to feel better. I was able to tune people out, and the rage I had was subsiding. My home life didn't get any better and neither did my job; it only got worst. When I would go to my doctor's appointments, my doctor would ask how I was feeling. I said, "I'm beginning to feel the same way I did when I first started coming to visit you, but now, I feel good at the beginning part of the day, and then, all of a sudden, my mood will swing, and I feel so low the second part of the day. The medication is not working." The doctor decided to increase the dosage of medication that I was already taking, and he put me on some new medication because of my mood swings. He said, "Garry, you have developed Bipolar Disorder. That's why I'm prescribing a new medication." It worked for a little while.

When I returned to work, I kept getting harassed by my captain over some evaluations, and one day, I snapped. I told the Captain that if he continued to harass me, I would take his white, narrow ass and throw him out of the window. As I looked at the Captain, my urge to kill him grew more and more. I called my doctor and told him what I was going to do to the captain, and he ordered me to leave work and come to his office. When I went to his office he said, "It's time for you to take some days off." I didn't want to take any days off; I wanted to carry out my plan. He said, "Garry, I can't allow you to leave my office with those thoughts in your mind; I rather for you to go in the hospital and rest." He gave me an ultimatum. "Either you volunteer to go in the hospital or I can Baker Act you - meaning I can order you to go to the hospital, without your permission, based on you saying that you are going to kill your captain. Garry, I rather for you to go in the hospital and rest."

I checked myself in the behavior center in Tallahassee reluctantly, but in the back of my mind, I said, "People are really going to label me now." Staff couldn't keep their mouths closed, and the inmates, who were suffering from mental illness, didn't have a clue of my illness. I used to hear inmates say that when I talked with them after being on suicide watch, they could feel that I understood them. They would say, "Lieutenant Jones, after we talk with you, we feel better." Little did they know, I was suffering from the same mental illness that they had.

I stayed in the hospital for one week; I felt good and returned back to work. It took two days of being back to work before I began to feel rage in my heart towards the captain. My ex-wife was constantly saying that I needed Jesus; she continued to nag me about Jesus. It wasn't what she was saying; it was how she was saying that I needed Jesus. She was trying to make me accept Jesus when I had already accepted him in my life. I had my own personal relationship with Jesus; it just wasn't the same relationship she had with Him. After looking back in retrospect, in my opinion, I think my ex-wife meant well when she encouraged me to depend on Jesus.

# CHAPTER 12

*Returning Back To Work Too Early*

The doctor warned me about returning back to work too soon. He stated that he didn't think it was wise to go back in the same hostile environment until I was completely well, and he was right. I had a follow-up appointment with my doctor ten days after I returned to work. I explained to the doctor that I had the same feeling about the captain; life would be better if I killed him. My doctor said, "Your depression has manifested itself into anger. Is there anywhere you can go to calm down, a place you love going and feel at peace?"

I said, "Washington, D.C." The doctor said to take two weeks off work and go and have some fun in Washington, D.C. I went to Washington D.C., where I had family and friends, and had a ball, but when I got on the plane to come back to Tallahassee, I had a bad anxiety attack. I didn't want to go back to the job, nor did I want to go home to be with my wife. My life was miserable.

After returning to the doctor for a third time, I told the doctor that my condition had gotten worse. He asked me if I had started drinking again; I told him no, and he knew I was lying. He ordered some blood work to be performed on me. According to the blood work, my liver showed that I had been drinking. I could look in my doctor's eyes and tell that he was beginning to get frustrated with me, and he said something that I think he had wanted to say all along. He said in a stern voice, "How can I heal you if you continue to go back to the same environment that is causing your problem in the first place? You are never going to get better if you continue to do that." My doctor told me three years prior that he wanted to retire me, but I refused, but this time, he said, "Garry, it's time for you to retire." I agreed.

After I agreed to retire, I called a family meeting with my children and explained to them what I was suffering from and why I had to retire. I gave my children the definition of depression and anxiety and the other mental illness that I suffered from. I asked my children if they had ever felt the way that I felt, and they said no. The reason I asked them those questions was because if one of them said yes, my plan was to immediately get them some help.

# CHAPTER 13

*Applying for Social Security Disability Benefits*

After retiring from the Federal Bureau of Prison I was told by Personnel that I had to apply for Disability. This was a long process that didn't help my mental state. As a matter of fact fighting to get your benefits can exacerbate an already fragile state of mind to downright despair. One would think if you leave from a hostile environment to start your life back over it would be easy but that was far from the truth.

I often think that once the government knows that you have a medical condition they will do their best to make it worst to the point of making a person contemplating suicide, then the government definitely wouldn't have to pay you anything. The Social Security Disability department had already had what they needed from two doctors stating that I couldn't work anymore but they wanted more. I guess they didn't believe what the doctors had to say. I submitted a letter from a friend who knew about my condition and how it affected me. I was going to ask my family to write a letter on my behalf but they didn't witness me going through the torment of depression.

# CHAPTER 14

*The Letter From A Friend*

*TO THE POWERS THAT BE:*

*As early as the dawn of this brand new day, Tuesday, April 14, 2009, I would receive one of the many similar calls received over the past twenty plus years from my lifelong friend, Garry Lamonte Jones. He was expressing his desire to not live life any longer as he now knows it. He would go on to divulge the "darkness of the life" he has lived for more than two decades, a life now described by many psychoanalytic experts as symptomatic of PTSD (Post Traumatic Stress Disorder). Jones, as some affectionately call him, has suffered greatly, and I have seen perhaps more of this suffering than most in his inner circle of friends and family.*

*Growing up in a small town of North Carolina, Garry had always been a "poster child," so we thought, not knowing he suffered from depression that had not been diagnosed or even recognized for that matter. He would always bear a smile that lit up any room he entered; however, few would come to really know the pain behind the smile. Jones was a walking misery, robed in garments that glittered as gold. Today, he lives his life secluded, for the most part, from the real world. On most days, Jones preferred to stay inside and gaze at the ceiling or sleep, hoping to awake and discover that this was all a nightmare, but to no avail, the suffering continues.*

*It was during Garry's tenure as an employee of the Federal Bureau of Prisons that I began to see signs of major depression. During this same time period, Garry was the victim of spousal abuse, both verbal and emotional/ mental, which plunged him further into the depths of utter frustration, bewilderment, etc., at his place of employment. Not to mention, the strife he endured while attempting to handle the challenges at work and home with someone who was determined, as vehemently as the powers on the job, to destroy the very fabric that somewhat held his life intact.*

*As far back as the year 2000, Garry began making visits to the state of Maryland where I, one of his closest confidantes, live to "get away" from the struggles of life at home with his wife and the job in Tallahassee, FL, but it only proved to get worse. For the most part, Jones would lodge at my dwelling where he always proclaimed to find peace in the midst of the storms of his depressive life. Having been hospitalized in early 2000 for this very depression, he resorted to my abode to recuperate, so he thought, only to find the condition worsening as he returned to his home and place of employment.*

*Jones would lose his most cherished aunt, with whom he stayed the last month or so of her life; this too would take a toll on my friend, lunging him into the abyss of deep sorrow and utter disgust with life on its terms. His beloved grandmother would depart this life not long after; the woman who was "muh" to Jones, having reared him to make the best of life, never giving up. His uncle, one who had assisted in his upbringing, would precede his grandmother in death by just a few months. By now, Jones has given up hope completely. He suffered a fall, as a result of passing out, on the day before news of his grandmother's grave illness and subsequent demise. He would have to undergo surgery on his left elbow and will soon have the same surgery on the right elbow.*

*Jones suffers much now, both mentally and physically. HIs kidneys are failing him, anxiety is at its highest peak, and his level of comprehension of even the simplest matters of importance has plummeted. Garry's love of family has always held HIGH esteem, but even his family now has its place. His children and grandchildren see a man constantly reaching out and helping them progress in life, not even having a clue that this man is in such inexplicable pain. He musters up the grace and courage to keep them unaffected; they too witnessed the abuse and only hoped for better for the man, their dad, who always went out of his way to make life grand for his posterity. Jones went through much turmoil at the news of denial of his Social Security benefits, which gave him a glimmer of hope of coming up out of this pit, enabling him to do some of the things he learned to love - advocating for the justice of the underprivileged, incarcerated citizens of our society.*

*He loved his Advocacy for Justice; now, he hardly speaks of the grassroots organization. He lost the fervor. He is constantly speaking of not wanting to live any longer; suicidal thoughts are prevalent indeed. We all wish we had our friend back. He has gone away, it seems, and I believe he can return if help is rendered both financially and medically.*

*Jones has pulled away, but I believe, as he once so firmly believed, that his study of the WORD has not really lost its savor. His spiritual life has suffered; "Be patient with Jones for God is not through with him yet." I am here to do all that I can to assist my friend in finding meaning in life again.*

*Humbly Submitted,*

*Lifelong friend of Garry Lamonte Jones*

# CHAPTER 15

*Life After Retirement*

I eventually separated from my wife and moved to Atlanta, but I would continue to go back to Tallahassee to see my kids and my doctor. When I would go to see my doctor, he would say, "Garry, how does it feel to be retired?" I told him that I didn't feel any better. He said, "How can you say that? You are no longer with your wife, and you are no longer working in that hostile environment."

I went on to explain to the doctor, "It's hard for me to feel better because I dream about what happened to me at the job, and I wake up sweating."

My doctor had this strange look on his face, and he said, "I was afraid this was going to happen. Garry, you are suffering from Post Traumatic Stress Disorder." I asked how I could be suffering from that when I had never been in the military. He said, "That's a misconception; you don't have to be in the military to suffer from a traumatic experience." He said, "Garry, you need counseling along with your medication. I want you to find a doctor in Atlanta and attend group therapy."

I said, "What about this PTSD?"

He said, "There is no cure for that disease, but it can be managed by medication and group therapy." I found a doctor in Atlanta, and a physician is still treating me today.

Later on in life, I would find out that my mother suffered from mental illness. I often think about what type of person I'd be if I didn't suffer from mental illnesses. Would I have made some decisions in life that I would come to regret? Did my illness keep me from being an A student; did my illness keep me from being a superb athlete rather than an average athlete? Would I have indulged in any drugs or alcohol for self-medication rather than recreation participation of getting high? Would I have been a better father, brother, uncle, boyfriend, husband, son, grandson, nephew, or even a better friend? I do know one thing; if I would have gotten help earlier in life, rather than being ashamed, I don't think I would be on medication, but I do think I would have been in therapy. I can't change the past, but I can make the future better for myself and everyone else. I'm a firm believer that a lot of our kids are suffering from some type of mental illness, and that is why they commit the crimes that they do. There are a lot of women and men who are promiscuous because they lack self-esteem. The only thing I know is that you owe it to yourself to get help; if not for yourself, do it for your family and friends because the decisions you make can be the downfall of someone else. Today, I am still trying to find other things that I can do to manage my depression, and I conduct seminars and speak about it on T.V.

# CHAPTER 16

*Managing Mental Illness*

I was told by one of my doctors that the road to recovery is accepting your condition. He said, "Once you accept your condition, you suffer less, and if you don't accept your condition, you suffer more." This statement may not sit well with the hardcore Christians; you know the type I'm referring to - the hardcore, bible toting, holier than thou Christians that don't believe in going to the doctor. The only thing that comes out of their mouth is you have to have faith. "Leave it to God, pray about it, and don't claim your condition." Half of the time when I hear those words, they go in one ear and out the other ear. The reason is that I don't feel their sincerity; hell, they don't feel their sincerity. As soon as they face a crisis, they don't follow the advice they give to you. I know the reason they talk the way they talk is because they take one scripture to hang their hat on and run with it; they don't take time to process what they are reading.

They forget to tell you faith without work is dead. They forget to tell you that things get done by fasting and praying and believing. I have been fasting and praying for the majority of my adult life. I have asked God to take the thorn, called depression, out of my side many times.

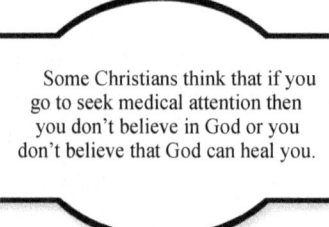

> Some Christians think that if you go to seek medical attention then you don't believe in God or you don't believe that God can heal you.

After I realized that he wasn't going to honor my request, I asked him to give me the strength to live with it without falling apart. It's a demon that I have to fight all the time. I have a problem with Christians questioning my faith.

Some Christians think that if you go to seek medical attention then you don't believe in God or you don't believe that God can heal you. That's a big lie, and people are dying every day because they believe that lie. God has put people in our paths to help manage our physical and mental health.

The other day, I was reading an article called *Rejecting Sickness* by Lee Underwood, and when I was reading it, he literally said the same thing I have always said when talking about the Bible toting Christians. He said it in a politically correct way, and I quote, "When told they're being attacked by a disease or suffering from sickness, many Christians reply, 'I refuse to accept that,' or something to that effect. The belief is that if they don't acknowledge ("accept") the sickness, then they will not be sick." There are literally thousands of Bible-toting Christians who believe and practice this concept.

This would give the appearance that it has a Biblical basis. Lee also gave talked about Scripture Healing, and he made great points to coincide with what I had been talking about the entire time. "The Scriptures are full of testimonies of healing provided by God through Jesus, the apostles, and many others. Through these healings, God was glorified in many ways. Generally, it was fairly simple: The person became sick, he acknowledged the attack he was suffering, he called out to the Lord, he believed the Lord would heal him, and he was healed." The next time a person tells you not to claim your illness, tell them to read Matthew 8:2. A leper came to Jesus and said, "Lord, if you are willing, you can make me clean," or, Mark 5:28; a woman, who had been hemorrhaging for twelve years, believed she would be healed if she could just touch Jesus' garment, and she was healed.

The healing begin when we first share it with someone - whether it is a friend, doctor, pastor, or someone you truly trust. If you find that this is hard to do, go somewhere and cry to release the pain. I heard someone say, "God created tear ducts for you to release the pain." Also, doing some type of physical exercise, getting plenty of rest, and changing your eating habits may be just what you need to begin to feel better. You will be amazed at how you will feel on the inside. If this doesn't work, then you may want to visit a doctor to receive some type of therapy. Therapy doesn't equate to medication, but if you choose to take medication, most doctors are going to administer low dosages, just to see how your body responds. After being on medication for a period of time, if you think you can manage your condition without medication, discuss it with your doctor. I'm aware that some physicians administer medication first, instead of recommending counseling, but as a patient, you have to take control of your health and manage it as well.

For those who suffer with mental illnesses, we have to know our triggers that exacerbate our condition. There are so many definitions for triggers, but I'm only naming one to get my point across. The verb trigger in the third person is a cause (an event or situation) to happen or exist. The synonyms are precipitate, set off, touch off, provoke, and stir up. My mental illness can be triggered by stress or overwork. In the next few chapters, I will discuss triggers that cause my mental illness to become worse. They include lack of exercise, lack of sleep, bad eating habits, associating with negative people, and Seasonal Affective Disorder. After you identify your triggers, it's important that you practice good mental health.

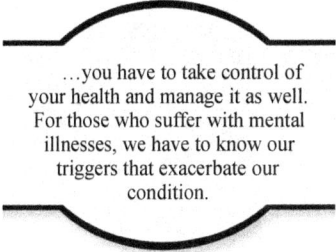

…you have to take control of your health and manage it as well. For those who suffer with mental illnesses, we have to know our triggers that exacerbate our condition.

*Pictures of Me Skydiving*

# CHAPTER 17

*TRIGGER #1:
Lack of Exercise*

For some reason, I think exercise helps with the depression. Without it, I don't think a person with depression can survive. I discovered this a long time ago when I was growing up. I have always been an athlete, and when I was not feeling well mentally, I knew that if I could just get to a gym or just walk a few miles by myself, I would feel a lot better. This may sound crazy but the hard part was getting out of bed when I was feeling depressed. I knew that if I got out of that house and did something, I would feel better. It's easier said than done because once you get in a funk, a simple task, like getting out of bed and putting one foot in front of the other, can be so damn hard. If you can make it outside and commence to doing some type of physical activity, even if you are shedding tears while you are doing it, you will notice the depression slowly begin to lift.

I don't know why exercise eases depression; maybe because after exercising for a short period of time, those endorphins kick in. Endorphins are any of a group of hormones secreted within the brain and nervous system, and they have a number of physiological functions. They are peptides that activate the body's opiate receptors, causing an analgesic effect. I always heard people talking about endorphins kicking in, and they said that once that happens, you will experience a natural high. I even heard of a phrase called *runner's high*. According to WebMD, "*runner's high* is a phrase that people use to describe the feelings of psychological well-being that are associated quite often with long-duration, rhythmic-type exercise."

Although I'm not a runner, I have been in the gym exercising, and I experienced euphoria and felt invincible. Once I feel that way, I don't want to leave the gym because I know it may be a long time before I feel that way again. I associate runner's high with what the Bible refers to as the peace of God, which surpasses all understanding, and you shall keep your hearts and mind on Christ Jesus. I don't feel this peace often, but when I do feel it, I try to relish in it. I wished I could bottle that peace up and drink some of it to make me feel better when I was feeling down.

Walking, running, and lifting weights are not the only exercises that make you feel good. There are other activities that ease depression - biking, dancing, swimming, gardening, yoga, playing tennis, going to Bible study, church, feeding the homeless, or mowing the lawn. As long as you are doing something, you will find yourself feeling better.

When I was a child, and sometimes as a young adult, and I was feeling sick, my grandmother would always say, "Garry, if you get up and stop lounging in bed and go outside on the porch, you will feel better. The longer you lie around the house, the worse you are going to feel." Although I thought I was too sick to get up, when I did get up and went outside to breathe in the fresh air, I felt a lot better. My grandmother always had the best remedies when I was sick.

# CHAPTER 18

*TRIGGER # 2:*
*Eating the Wrong Foods*

The older I get, the more I'm beginning to realize that eating the wrong foods can add to one's depression. Growing up, my grandmother always prepared a healthy, nutritious meal, but I didn't eat it. As a matter of fact, when she ordered me to sit at the kitchen table for dinner and eat collard greens, green beans, tomatoes, rice, fish, cornbread, and neck bones, I refused to eat it. Of course, when she cooked fried chicken or pork chops with homemade mashed potatoes, I would eat. Sometimes, I would put the collard greens in my mouth and then ask to be excused to go and use the restroom. When I got to the restroom, I would spit the collards in the toilet.

I was a junk food junky. The foods I ate the most were cereal, burnt bologna, candy, cake, and ice cream. I didn't care for fruits; maybe I would eat an orange every now and then. I would only eat bananas whenever my grandmother would put them in her famous banana pudding. I couldn't tolerate eggs, grits, and oatmeal, but I loved the hell out of some bacon on breakfast toast with jelly. As a kid, I was very sick mentally and physically. No one in my family knew about the mental sickness. After my grandmother realized that I wasn't going to eat the nutritious foods, she carried me to the doctor, and I was prescribed vitamins. I only took them when she gave them to me; I never took them on my own.

When I went off to college, it was the same routine. I constantly ate junk food, and I had money to order a pepperoni and sausage pizza from Godfather's Pizza three days a week. Sometimes, I would order pizza two times a day. After moving into my apartment, I would cook spaghetti at least twice a week. I loved Italian food. After I left college, I moved back home for a short period of time. My grandmother was still cooking the same nutritious meals, and I began to eat fruits and vegetables and baked foods. A change started taking place. I noticed that when I had a full course meal, I wasn't as hungry, but when I ate junk food, I stayed hungry. After several years of eating the right foods, I noticed that I wasn't as depressed as much. I wasn't healed, but I could feel a difference mentally. My grandmother was excited that I was taking care of myself in the food department.

I also noticed that when I ate a full course meal, I didn't feel as weighed down. I tried not to allow myself to become full. I don't know whether or not eating healthy food had anything to do with me feeling good mentally, but I can't help but believe that there is a direct correlation with eating healthy food and being less depressed. Maybe it was in my mind, but I'm convinced that eating healthy helps with your mental state of mind. I noticed that as soon as I began to eat junk food again or go on an alcohol binge, I would feel very depressed.

I'm a firm believer that what we eat can determine how we feel, but how we feel can determine what we eat. I'm a living witness. When I'm feeling low on energy and sluggish, I feel terrible, and I will result to eating unhealthy food, but when I have a lot of energy, I don't want unhealthy food. There is an old saying, "Junk in, junk out," meaning that whatever you put in your system is what you are going to get out of it. If you put junk food in your system, it is going to have a negative effect on how you feel. I'm not saying never to eat junk food again; what I'm saying is to try not to each much of it. I believe that the body is not designed to deprive you of nutrition. A person who suffers from depression shouldn't go on a crash diet unless you are getting the proper nutrients. Crash diets throw your body's chemistry off because of the lack of nutrients your body needs. You are only setting yourself up to be more depressed.

I believe that if we stick to the dietary pyramid, we are less likely to feel as depressed because our bodies are getting the proper nutrition. The older we get, the more our bodies change, and we can't consume some of the foods on the dietary pyramid as much. The dietary pyramid consists of five groups – the dairy group (two servings), vegetable group (three to five servings), protein (two to three servings), fruit group, (two to four servings), and the grains group (six to eleven servings).

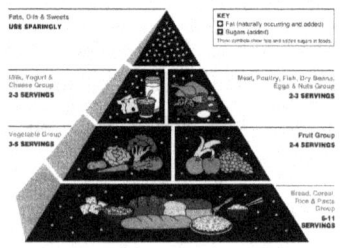

# CHAPTER 19

*TRIGGER # 3:
Lack of Sleep*

I was never big on sleep, not because I didn't want to, but because I just couldn't sleep more than five hours maximum. I don't care what time I would go to sleep, I would still be up early in the morning. I have been this way since I was a kid. Did you know that a lack of sleep can cause depression? It has taken me forty-five years to figure out that the lack of sleep, the lack of exercise, the lack of nutritional meals, and hanging around negative people will either cause you to go into a depression, or if you are already depressed, it will cause you to stay in a depressed state. I'm beginning to learn a lot about my disease that I should have learned a long time ago.

Sometimes, I feel like a fool. I wish I would have accepted that I had depression, and I wish I would have studied my disease to find out the do's and don'ts in managing my depression. I think I would have been able to manage it a lot better, just like I manage my asthma. It's amazing how we can accept that we have a physical illness, but when it comes to accepting a mental illness, we hide it because we know how society is going to label us. The hell with society; I have a mental illness, and I'm trying very hard to live with the condition, but knowing what sets you off, like a lack of sleep, makes life a lot easier.

It was only a couple of years ago that I figured out that a lack of sleep triggers my depression. Sometimes, I could go to bed feeling great, but I would wake up very depressed. I couldn't figure out what was going on, knowing that I had good thoughts the night before I went to bed. 'Why am I depressed?' I would ask myself. I began to notice that whenever I grew tired or didn't sleep well, I would wake up depressed. Although the doctor had put me on sleep medication when I had insomnia, I still didn't sleep well. In May 2013, I had gone to several events, including a graduation, and I didn't sleep for twenty-four hours. This was during Mother's Day weekend. I remember going to sleep Saturday night before Mother's Day, thinking about my grandmother, but I had a peace that came over me. I was smiling before I went to sleep, and the next day I awakened, depressed.

I got out of bed to go to church, and I was baffled about being depressed because I was feeling great prior to me going to sleep. Then, I had an epiphany. I figured out what had happened and why I was depressed. I had stayed up running around and having fun for over twenty-four hours, and my body was very tired. The fact that I didn't sleep well brought on this enormous depression. I came to the conclusion that I couldn't afford to allow myself to get very tired and stay up for over twenty-four hours because I will fall in that funk.

Today, I sleep with a sleep apnea machine because I snore, and when a person snores, they stop breathing, and when you stop breathing, there is not enough oxygen going to the brain. This causes your sleep to be interrupted. It's normal for me to wake up three times a night, but with my machine, I don't wake up as often. I was told by my doctors that sleeping with a sleep apnea machine can help manage depression because my sleep was not being interrupted, and my body feels fresh, not sluggish, when I awaken.

# CHAPTER

# 20

*TRIGGER # 4:*
*Associating With Negative People*

Last but not least, continuing to fellowship with people who are always complaining and who always have negative things to say, about every situation, will cause a person who suffers from depression to continue to be in a depressed state of mine. Has anyone ever called you on the telephone, and when you picked it up to have a conversation, you were in a good mood, but when you hung up from talking to that person, you noticed that your mood went from good to bad? You may have not noticed this on the first four or five times that you talked with that person, but eventually, you begin to say to yourself, "Every time I get through having a conversation with this person, I feel depressed." The reason is because one can't continue to be around negative people for a long period of time without eventually feeling depressed.

Although it has taken me some time to figure what works for me and what doesn't work for me, it has made a big difference in my mental state of mind. When a person calls me on the telephone and I know that this person is going to talk about negative things and complain a lot, I don't answer my phone. I try to stay as far away from them as possible. In order to change our current situation, we have to be willing to give up people, places, and things that alter our mood. This is not being selfish; this is being smart. I don't have a problem listening to a friend in need, but when that friend or family member complains ninety-five percent of the time, it's time to back away from that person.

Never share your ideas with negative people because they will try to find a way of convincing you that the idea is not going to work. I don't think negative people even realize that they are being negative. They may be great people, but they are always looking at the glass half empty. Their self-defeating thoughts can reduce your confidence and cause you to become very depressed. Anytime someone is always saying you can't, you are not good enough, you don't have what it takes, and you are going to fail, it's time to leave those self-defeating people alone. Sometimes negative people are jealous of you and your success, although they had the same opportunities that you had in life. The difference is that they chose not to do anything with their life, while you chose to do something positive with your life. Sometimes, those negative people had better opportunities to succeed in life because their social economic statuses were better than yours, they were more popular than you, their parents gave them everything, and you had to work for everything.

On another note, we have to be careful of the things we listen to because listening to depressing music can cause you to stay in a depressed state of mind. Take for an example, during Christmas, I love to listen to a song, by a group called The Emotions, called '*What Do the Lonely do for Christmas?* It's a very beautiful song, but I find myself going deeper and deeper into my depression. Don't get me wrong, I love listening to love songs, but I also have to mix it up with some fast songs to keep my mental state balanced. Too much of anything is not good for you, and not enough of the right things aren't good for you either. Balance is the key if you want to live a healthy life mentally.

Last but not least, I love watching the news on television. My family knows that I don't watch a lot of shows because I love politics, and I want to be informed on what's going on in this world, and looking at the news can give me what I need. One day, I was in my hometown in Kinston, N.C., and I was looking at Cable News Network (CNN). About two hours later, I was still looking at CNN. My brother asked me, "Why do you continue to look at the same news over and over? They are going to show you the same thing every thirty minutes." I told him that I just loved looking at the news. If you find yourself doing too much of one thing that is negative, it may not be good for you. I love looking at the news, but today, most of the news is negative news. There are wars, police brutality, rape, murder, child molestation, rioting in the streets, missing children, kidnapping, and etc. My mind is consuming too many negative things on the news. Although I'm a serious person, now I have to watch funny things. I have to go to the park instead of staying in the house all day; I have to find a way to give my life the proper balance, and I'm a work in process. I have learned the things that keep my spirits low, and now I have to practice what I preach in order to maintain good mental health.

# CHAPTER 21

*TRIGGER:#5*
*Seasonal Affective Disorder*

I noticed that some people only get depressed during different seasons of the year. It's similar to anniversaries, holidays, and birthdays of dead relatives, but it lasts only a season. Some people only get depressed during the fall and winter months, when there is not a lot of light. This is called Seasonal Affective Disorder (SAD). According to the Mayo Clinic staff definition, "This is a type of depression that's related to changes in seasons. SAD begins and ends at about the same time every year. If you are like most people with SAD, your symptoms start in the fall and continue into the winter months, sapping your energy, and making you feel moody. Less often, SAD causes depression in the spring or early summer.

"Treatment for SAD may include light therapy, psychotherapy, and medications. Don't brush off that yearly feeling as simply a case of the "winter blues" or a seasonal funk that you have to tough out on your own. Take steps to keep your mood and motivation steady throughout the year."

I'm not sure whether or not I suffer from SAD, but I don't like my blinds open. I can recall plenty of times when I was home in North

Carolina, my Aunt Denderaunt would come over to the house and say, "Boy, open these blinds. Why are you sitting in the house with the blinds closed when it's sunny outside?" I never had an answer for my aunt, but I wanted to say, "What's wrong with me having the blinds closed?" I wouldn't dare say that. On the other hand, my Aunt Mavis would open the blinds without saying anything when I was in the house. I really don't want to make a big deal out of SAD because I don't think I suffer from the disorder, but it is something to think about. OPEN YOUR MIND AND LET THE SUNSHINE IN!!!!!!

# CHAPTER 22

*Learning to
Accept The Things You Can't
Change*

If one is suffering from depression, their mind has to remain positive. This is hard to do with so many negative distractions going on in this world. You don't have the luxury of getting upset over things you can't control. For an example, the average person is hurt to the core when they suffer a loss of a precious loved one, especially losing a relative who raised you. I remember when I lost my Aunt Arnetta, and then, two years later, I lost my Uncle Earl. Three months after that, I would lose the love of my life, my grandmother, Mrs. Tessie Jones. I was devastated! When the anniversary of their death or the holidays came around, I would dread it. I could feel myself going into a deep depression, a depression that would be hard for me to recover or come out of.

It is a natural thing to feel the way I felt, being depressed on the anniversary of a loved one's death. There is nothing we can do as a human to reverse those dates or holidays because they come around once a year. I knew my heart was going to be hurting once those days came around, but I also knew that I had to do something about it. I began to think of great things or laugh about things I used to hear my loves say while they were living. This put me in a positive mindset. There are a lot of things we can do when the anniversary of our loved one's death comes around. For example, my grandmother used to love watching the soap opera, *The Young and the Restless*. This year, when the anniversary of her death comes around, I will be looking at *The Young and the Restless*. Try to do things that they loved doing, and I can guarantee that you will feel much better.

# CHAPTER 23

*The Importance of Practicing Good Mental Health*

Practicing good mental health is just as important as the practice of good physical health and diet. One's body can be in the best physical shape, but if the mind is not in the same place, it can be rather destructive.

We live in a fast-paced, pressure filled society that demands more than our minds may be able to handle. With this in mind, it behooves everyone to breathe the fresh air in nature. Find something you love and engross yourself in it. Do the things you dreamed of doing. I always dreamed about going skydiving. After I discovered that I had prostate cancer in 2010 and having surgery in 2011, I decided to pick something on my bucket list and make it a reality. Skydiving is no longer on my bucket list, and if I had money to skydive every day, I would do it.

The next thing on my bucket list is to fly a plane. Not only was jumping out of the plane fun, but I want to know how it is to fly one. If it is God's will, I'm going to fly a plane. Eighteen years ago, when I was staying in Tallahassee, I discovered a place where they teach you how to fly planes. I wish I would have taken flying lessons, but although I didn't, it's never too late to learn how to fly. If you are in good mental and physical health, you can achieve anything you want, depending on how bad you want it and how much work you are willing to put in to get it.

# CHAPTER 24

*Removing the Stigma*

People have been crying out for help for a long time, and we, the people in the public, ridicule those who have been acting out. Take for an example, as soon as we see a tragic event on television, such as mass shootings at a school, movie theater, military base, or nightclub, domestic violence, workplace violence, or people taking their own lives, then we want to speak out. After witnessing something tragic, most of us say, "I thought something was strange about that individual." If that is the case, why in the hell didn't you speak out then? If a person goes to seek help for their mental illness, the public ridicules them, and when a person doesn't go to seek help and goes out and commits unthinkable crimes or kills themselves, the first thing the public says is, "He or she should have gone out to get some help for their mental condition." You are damned if you do and damned if you don't. I do believe in my heart that there is a correlation between violence, suicide, and someone who suffers from poor mental health.

Mental illness has been flying under the radar for a long time. In the United States, we never wanted to address the issue, and I'm sure the enemy (Satan) is laughing because he has stolen so many souls due to mental illnesses. Our attention has been diverted to something else. The suicide rate is skyrocketing, and people have been killing other people in droves, but we could never figure out why. There has never been enough resources delegated to treat mental illnesses. Our resources have been depleted on fighting wars such as Vietnam, Gulf, Iraq, and the war on drugs.

# Epilogue

If you suffer from mental illness and you refuse to get help, there is a heavy price one has to pay. Something so small can turn into something so big if you don't get help.

## *THE PRICE I HAD TO PAY FOR NOT GETTING HELP SOONER*

If you suffer from mental illness and you refuse to get help, there is a heavy price one has to pay. Something so small can turn into something so big if you don't get help. Take for example, if you have diabetes and you mistakenly cut yourself - in your mind you are thinking it's a small cut; you put alcohol on it and maybe a Band-Aid and think everything is going to be fine, but in a couple of months, you realize that the cut is not healing. You decide to go to the doctor because your wound is not healing, but when you get there, the doctor tells you gangrene has set in on the wound, and they have the amputate your finger. This is what I mean when I say that if an illness left untreated, something so small can cause you major problems in the future.

A person who suffers from mental illness struggles to get out of the dark, but in order to obtain the light you must embrace the darkness inside of you.

I truly believe that if I would have gotten treatment for my depression in its early stages, I may have been healed, *Still I Rise*!

www.ingramcontent.com/pod-product-compliance
Lightning Source LLC
Chambersburg PA
CBHW070624300426
44113CB00010B/1648